RULES OF THUMB

A Guide for Writers

RULES OF THUMB

A Guide for Writers

Jay Silverman
Nassau Community College

Elaine Hughes
Nassau Community College

Diana Roberts Wienbroer
Nassau Community College

McGraw-Hill Publishing Company

New York   St. Louis   San Francisco   Auckland   Bogotá
Caracas   Hamburg   Lisbon   London   Madrid   Mexico   Milan
Montreal   New Delhi   Oklahoma City   Paris   San Juan
São Paulo   Singapore   Sydney   Tokyo   Toronto

1 2 3 4 5 6 7 8 9 0 DOC DOC   9 4 3 2 1 0

ISBN 0-07-057548-7
ISBN 0-07-057564-9 (Trade Edition)

This book was set in Palatino by J. M. Post Graphics, Corp.
The editors were Lesley Denton and David Dunham;
the designer was Merrill Haber;
the production supervisor was Janelle S. Travers.
R. R. Donnelley & Sons Company was printer and binder.

Library of Congress Cataloging-in-Publication Data is Available
LC Card #89-38886

ACKNOWLEDGMENTS

For their careful reading and questioning of various drafts of *Rules of Thumb*, we wish to thank Beverly Jensen; Polly Marshall, Hinds Community College; Nell Ann Pickett, Hinds Community College; and Larry Richman, Virginia Highlands Community College.

We also appreciate the thoughtful comments of Diana Cox, Amarillo College; Ralph G. Dille, University of Southern Colorado; Kathryn Tripp Feldman, Nassau Community College; Bernice Kliman, Nassau Community College; Mary McFarland, Fresno City College; Retta Porter, Hinds Community College; Sara L. Sanders, Coastal Community College; A. Gordon Van Ness III, Longwood College; and Dominick Yezzo, Nassau Community College. We are grateful for the encouragement and enthusiasm of our colleagues in the English Department at Nassau Community College.

This book would not have existed but for our students—both as the audience we had in mind and as perceptive readers and critics.

CONTENTS

PART III: PUTTING A PAPER TOGETHER

PART IV: WRITING WITH ELEGANCE

HOW TO USE RULES OF THUMB

This book is for you if you love to write, but it's also for you if you *have* to write. *Rules of Thumb* is a quick reference guide that reduces each writing problem to a few practical points. You can use it easily, on your own, and feel confident in your writing.

We suggest that you read *Rules of Thumb* in small doses, out of order, when you need it. It's not like a novel that keeps you up late into the night. You'll need to read a few lines and then pause to see if you understand. After ten minutes, set the book aside. From time to time, look at the same points again as a reminder.

The book has four parts. Part I, "Correctness," covers the most common mistakes. We put these rules first because they are what most students worry about and will want to have handy. However, when you are writing your ideas, don't get distracted with correctness; afterwards, take the time to look up the rules you need. Part II, "Meeting Specific Assignments," offers help with writing under time pressure and with writing reports. Part III, "Putting a Paper Together," will help you with both content and style—if you're stuck, if you need to make a paper longer, or if you have choppy sentences. Part IV, "Writing with Elegance," offers ways to grow as a writer. You won't necessarily use these parts in order because the process of writing does not follow a set sequence. Generating ideas, organizing, revising, and correcting all happen at several points along the way.

Rules of Thumb doesn't attempt to cover every little detail of grammar and usage, but it does cover the most common problems we've seen as teachers of writing over the past twenty years. We chose the phrase "rules of thumb" because it means a quick guide. The top part of your thumb is roughly an inch long. Sometimes you need a ruler, marked in millimeters, but sometimes you can do fine by measuring with just your thumb. Your thumb takes only a second to use, and it's always with you. We hope you'll find *Rules of Thumb* just as easy and comfortable to use.

Jay Silverman
Elaine Hughes
Diana Roberts Wienbroer

RULES OF THUMB

A Guide for Writers

CORRECTNESS

P·A·R·T I

A WORD ABOUT CORRECTNESS

Too much concern about correctness can inhibit your writing; too little concern can come between you and your readers. Don't let the fear of errors dominate the experience of writing for you. On the other hand, we would be misleading you if we told you that correctness doesn't matter. Basic errors in writing will distract and turn off even the most determined readers. We encourage you to master these few rules as quickly as possible so that you can feel secure about your writing. Once that happens, you'll be free to concentrate on what you want to say.

CONFUSING WORDS

These words are used all the time, so you need to know them. Find the ones that give you trouble and learn those.

a	Use before words starting with consonant sounds or long *u* (a bat, a cat, a union).
an	Use before words starting with vowels or pronounced as if they did (an age, an egg, an hour, an M&M).
accept	To take, to receive I gladly accept your praise.
except	Not including Everyone except Noah voted yes.
affect	To change or influence Starlight affects us in ways we don't understand.
effect	The result, the consequence *Effect* is usually a noun, so you'll find *the* or *an* in front. We are studying the effects of starlight on human beings.
etc.	Abbreviation of *et cetera*, which means "and so forth" in Latin. The *t* is in the middle. The *c* is at the end, followed by a period. Don't write *and etc*. We bought confetti, serpentine, fireworks, etc., for the party.

good, well	Test by trying your sentence with both. If *well* fits, use it. He plays third base well. He is a good third baseman.
it's	It is. Test by substituting *it is.* It's easy.
its	Possessive Every goat is attached to its own legs. No apostrophe. *It is* cannot be substituted.
lay	To put something down *-ing:*　　　She is laying out the facts. *Past Tense:*　He laid the book on the table. Once you *lay* something down, it *lies* there.
lie	To recline Lie down. Past tense (here's the tricky part): *lay.* Yesterday I lay down for half an hour.
loose	Not tight After he lost thirty pounds, his jeans were all loose.
lose	To misplace I constantly lose my glasses. To be defeated I win; you lose.
No, new, now, know, knew	No is negative; *new* is not old; *now* is the present moment. *Know* and *knew* refer to knowledge.
of, have	Remember: *could have, should have, would have,* not *would of.*

passed	A course, a car, a football; also, *passed away* (*died*)
	Kirtley passed me on the street; he also passed English.
	Saturday he passed for two touchdowns.
	The coach passed away.
past	Yesterdays (the past; past events); also, *beyond*
	He can never forget his past romances.
	You can't live in the past.
	Go two miles past the railroad tracks.
quiet	He is the quiet type.
quit	She quit her job the day she won the lottery.
quite	The monkeys are quite noisy today.
than	Comparison
	I'd rather dance than eat.
then	Next
	And then it happened.
their	Something is theirs.
	You hurt their feelings.
there	*A place:* Go over there.
	There is . . . *There* are . . . *There* was . . . *There* were
	There are a thousand reasons why I fear her.
they're	They are.
	They're hard to handle.
to	*Direction:* Give it to me. Go to New York.
	A verb form: To see, to run, to be.
	(Note that you barely pronounce *to.*)
too	*Very:* Too hot, too bad, too late, too much.
	Also: Me, too!
	(Note that you pronounce *too* clearly.)
two	2

were	*Past Tense*: You were, we were, they were.
we're	*We Are*: We're as silly as we can be.
where	*A Place*: Where were you?
whether	Not *weather*—rain or snow Tell me whether or not you love me.
who's	*Who is*: Who's there? Who's coming with us?
whose	*Possessive*: Whose diamond is this?
women	Several of them. This woman is different from all other women. Don't write *a women*!
your	Belonging to you. Use only for your house, your car—*not* when you mean *you are*.
you're	You are. You're handsome.

ONE WORD OR TWO?

If you can put another word between them, you'll know to keep them separate. Otherwise, you'll have to check them one by one.

a lot	I like you a lot—a whole lot. (*A lot* is always written as two words.)
all ready	We were all ready for Grandpa's wedding.
already	Helen already has plans for Saturday.
all right	It's all right with me if you want to quit.
a long	Childhood seems like a long time.
along	Come along to the carnival.
a part	I want a part of the American pie.
apart	Even when we're apart, I think of you.
everybody	Everybody in the room danced to the music.
every day	It rains every day, every single day.
everyday	I put on my everyday clothes.
every one	He ate every one of the cookies—every last one.
everyone	Everyone likes pizza.
in depth	Study the biology textbook in depth.
in fact	In fact, Janine wasn't in the room when the ruckus started.
in order	In order to prove her point, Marty climbed onto the desk.

in spite of	I like you in spite of your churlish disposition.
into	Ann Appleton fell into an easy job.
itself	The cat sunned itself.
myself	I fixed the car myself.
no one	No one ever calls me anymore.
nowadays	Nowadays, they call ice boxes "refrigerators."
nevertheless	Nevertheless, Billy's in for a tough campaign.
some time	I need some time alone.
sometimes	Sometimes I get the blues.
somehow	Somehow the laundry never gets done.
throughout	Throughout the entire summer, David lounged on the beach.
whenever	Whenever I hear that song, I start to cry.
whereas	I'm always on time, whereas my brother is always late.
wherever	Wherever Lillian goes, she goes in style.
withheld	Joe withheld the rent because the roof leaked.
without	You'll never catch Pearl without her sunglasses.

SPELLING

Even if you consider yourself a poor speller, these tips will get you through most spelling problems.

I Before E

I before *E* except after *C*
Or when sounded like *A*,
As in *neighbor* and *weigh*.

bel*i*eve	dece*i*ve
fr*i*end	rece*i*ve
p*i*ece	

Word Endings

- The quiet *-ed* endings: three *-ed* endings are not always pronounced, but they need to be written.

  used to
  supposed to
  prejudiced

- *St-sk* endings: when *s* is added to words like these, it isn't always pronounced, but it still needs to be there.

asks	consists	psychologists
risks	insists	scientists
desks	suggests	terrorists

- The *-ing* endings: when a word ends in *y*, keep the *y* when you add *ing*. To add *-s* or *ed*, change the *y* to *i*.

crying	cries	cried
studying	studies	studied
trying	tries	tried

- The *-ly* endings: don't change the word; just add *ly*.

  really   totally   lonely

  But *truly* is the exception.

- *P* or *pp*? *T* or *tt*?
  Listen to the *vowel before* the added part. If the vowel sounds like its own letter name, use only one consonant:

  writer   writing

  The *i* sounds like the name of the letter *i*, so you use one *t*.
  If the vowel before the added part has a different sound from its name, you *double the consonant*:

  written

  The *i* sounds like the *i* in *it*, so you double the *t*.
  Here are some other examples:

  beginning   dropping
  stopped   occurred

  An exception: coming

Tricky Words

definitely   probably   separate
interest   repetition   usually
opinion

ABBREVIATIONS AND NUMBERS

When in doubt, spell it out.

ABBREVIATIONS

- As a general rule, don't abbreviate—especially don't use abbreviations like these in papers:

dept.	yr.	NY	Eng.	Thurs.
w/o	co.	&	gov't.	Prof.

- But do abbreviate words which you *always* see abbreviated—such as certain titles with proper names and well-known organizations:

Mr. Smith	FBI
St. Bartholomew	IBM

- Abbreviate Dr. *only* before a name:

  | The doctor | Dr. Salk |

NUMBERS

Spell out

Numbers that take only one or two words

| nine | twenty-seven | two billion |

Numbers that begin a sentence

One hundred and four years ago the ship sank.
The ship sank 104 years ago.

Numbers that form a compound word

a two-year-old baby

Fractions

one-half

Use Numerals for

Numbers that require three or more words

1,889   162

Dates, page references, room numbers, percentages, statistics, and addresses

1889   7,500 residents   99.44%

page 2   221 B Baker Street

A list or series of numbers

1, 4, 9, 16, 25

APOSTROPHES

Most of the time, when you add an *s* to a word, you don't need an apostrophe. Use apostrophes for contractions and possessives.

Add an Apostrophe

- To a contraction (put the apostrophe where the missing letter was)

doesn't = does not	it's = it is	that's
don't	I'm	weren't
didn't	you're	what's

- To a possessive

John's hat	men's room	a night's sleep
Ms. Jones's opinion	women's room	today's world
Baldwin's sentences	people's feelings	

  If the word is plural and already ends with *s*, just add an apostrophe after the *s*.

  my friends' apartment (*several friends*)

  But note: Pronouns in possessive form have *no* apostrophe.

  its   hers   his   ours   theirs   yours

Do Not Add an Apostrophe; Just Add s or es

- To make a plural

  Two bosses
  Three dogs

- To a present-tense verb

  He sees.   Look hard at *sees* and *says*: no apostrophe.
  She says.
  It talks.

CONSISTENT PRONOUNS

Make a conscious choice of your pronouns. Don't shift from *a person* to *they* to *you* to *I*.

Avoid writing sentences like,

I got mad; it does make you feel upset when people don't listen.

or

If a person wants success, they have to have connections.

Here are the choices:

a person
someone

These words can lead to awkward writing and create errors

If a person is strong, they will stand up for themselves.
I know someone rich, and they are not very happy.

Note that *a person* and *someone* are singular; *they* is plural. Instead of *a person* or *someone*, use *people* (which fits with *they*).

If people are strong, they will stand up for themselves.

Or, better yet, use a true-to-life example, a real person:

My cousin Marc is strong: he stands up for himself.

A real example not only makes the grammar correct, but it is much more interesting and memorable. *A person* and *someone* are nobodies.

he
he or she

The old-fashioned choice to go with *a person* would be *he*:

> If a person is strong, he will stand up for himself.

But this choice presumes that *a person* is male. It should be avoided because it is sexist language. *He or she* is possible, but not if it comes several times in a row:

> If a person is strong, he or she will stand up for himself or herself.

He or she, when repeated, becomes clunky and awkward. *He/she* is not much better. The best solution, usually, is to use *people* and *they*.

I

Don't be afraid of *I*. It is very strong in writing about emotions and experience. In these matters, being *objective* is not as good as being *truthful*. As Thoreau says, "I should not talk so much about myself if there were anybody else whom I knew as well." You don't, however, need phrases like *I think* or *in my opinion* because the whole paper is, after all, what *you* choose to say.

you

You is good for giving directions and writing letters. For essays, it may seem too informal.

Try *we* instead, when you mean *people in general*.

> If you're strong, you stand up for yourself.
> If we are strong, we stand up for ourselves.

In any case, beware of sentences like

Riding my bicycle is good for your legs.

one

One means *a person*—singular. If you use it, you must stick with it:

If one is strong, one stands up for oneself.

One is an option for solving the he/she problem; it is appropriate for formal writing. Nevertheless, when repeated, *one* can sound stuffy. How many times can one say *one* before one makes oneself sound silly?

we

We can be used to mean *people in general.*

If we are strong, we stand up for our rights.

Be careful that you mean more than just yourself. Using *I* might be more appropriate.

they

They is the best solution to the *he/she* problem, but remember that *they* must refer to a plural, such as *many people* or *some people.*

CORRECT PRONOUNS (I VS. ME)

I, she, he, we, they describe the persons doing the action. *Me, her, him, us, them* describe the persons receiving the action.

Pairs: My friends and I / My friends and me

With a pair of people, try the sentence without the other person:

My friends and *I* went to the movies.
(. . . I went to the movies, *not* Me went to the movies.)

He gave the tickets to my friends and me.
(He gave the tickets to me, *not* to I.)

The same rule goes for *him, her, he, she.*

We sued her father and her.
(We sued her, *not* We sued she.)

Note: Put *yourself* last in a list:

My friends and I . . .
Beverly gave pumpkin cake to Noah and me.

Don't be afraid of *me;* it's often right.

Let's keep this between you and me.
(*not* . . . between you and I.)

Don't use *myself* when *me* will do.

Sam did the typing for Toby and me.
(Not . . . for Toby and myself.)

Comparisons

Use *I, he, she, we, they* when comparing with the subject of the sentence—usually the first person in the sentence.

Phil was kinder to Sarah than I was.
John is sweeter than she is.

Sometimes *is* is left off the end:

John is sweeter than she.

Use *me, him, her, us, them* when comparing with the receiver, the object of the sentence—usually the person mentioned later in the sentence.

Phil was kinder to Sarah than to me.

Note the difference:

He was nastier to Bill than I.   (He was nastier to Bill than I was.)
He was nastier to Bill than me.   (He was nastier to Bill than to me.)

VAGUE PRONOUNS: WHICH, IT, THIS, THAT, AND WHO

Certain pronouns—*which, it, this, that,* and *who*—must refer to a single word, not to a whole phrase.

Which

Which causes the most trouble of the five. Get rid of *which* as often as possible. Save it for questions.

Which kind of sandwich would you like?

Imprecise: I felt sick last week which I didn't even get to go to school.

Precise: I felt sick last week. I didn't even get to go to school.

Use *in which* only when you mean that one thing is inside the other:

The box in which I keep my jewelry fell apart.

It

When you use *it*, make sure the reader knows what *it* is. *It* is often weak at the start of a sentence when *it* refers to nothing.

Imprecise: It is sad to see Granny so sick.
Precise: I feel sad to see Granny so sick.

This

This cannot refer to a whole situation or a group of things, so insert a word after *this* to sum up what *this* refers to.

Imprecise:	She never calls me, she's never ready when I pick her up for a date, and she forgot my birthday. This makes me angry.
Precise:	She never calls me, she's never ready when I pick her up for a date, and she forgot my birthday. This neglect makes me angry.

That

That refers to things, not people.

The car that I bought Wednesday is already in the shop.

Who

Use *who* for people—not *which* or *that*.

The runner who finished last got all the publicity.

Use *whom* after prepositions (to whom, of whom, from whom, with whom).
When in doubt, use *who*.

RUN-ON SENTENCES AND FRAGMENTS

When you're not sure whether to use a period or a comma, look at the word that comes next to see if it is a sentence starter or a sentence connector.

Often you reach a pause and you wonder, "Do I put a comma or a period?" The length of the sentence has nothing to do with the right choice. Here is a system to help you decide.

When you reach a pause, look at the *next* few words. If the next word is an obvious *sentence connector* (*but, so, which*), you keep going—no period. However, if the next word is a typical *sentence starter*, such as *it* or *I*, you probably have a new sentence, and you need a period.

RUN-ON SENTENCES

Remember, you must use a period even between very short but complete sentences:

It was a rainy Monday. I was sitting at my desk. I heard a knock at the door. I waited. The doorknob turned.

Learn the typical *sentence starters*:

It is (It's)	The dog ran
He said	New York is
She was	Mary has
I believe	We didn't
They were	

Note the noun-verb pattern. Most sentences start this way. To avoid run-on sentences, look at the words that follow the pause. If you see a sentence starter, use a period.

Sometimes you'll have a word or phrase before the *sentence starter*—a lead-in.

> However, the bar is closed.
> Therefore, we are planning a trip to the moon.
> For example, Mona screams when she talks.
> Then we drove a thousand miles.
> If you need a ride, Harry can take you.
> When James walked in, the whole family was laughing hysterically.

The two most common spots for run-ons are

- When a pronoun begins the second sentence:

> Tabby was running around the yard. She fell into a hole.
> The light floated toward us. It gave an eerie glow.

- When *however* begins the second sentence:

> She says she loves me. However, she doesn't show it.

A fine point:
You can use a *semicolon* instead of a period if the two complete sentences have a close connection.

> I love ice cream; it's refreshing.
> I love ice cream; however, it's fattening.

SENTENCE FRAGMENTS

- Here are the most common *sentence connectors*. They usually do not start sentences:

and	yet	like
but	such as	just like
or	especially	the same as
so		not

which
who
whose } (except in a question)
how
what

- Certain other words can start a sentence, but it will be a *two-part sentence*. The following words begin only half a sentence, which can be the first half or the second half.

when	because
after	if
before	although
while	though
as	unless
since	whereas

By itself, the half with one of these words is a fragment. Fix this fragment by joining it to the sentence before it or the sentence after it.

Fragment: I could lose weight. If I ran home every day.

Correct: I could lose weight if I ran home every day.

Correct: If I ran home every day, I could lose weight.

Here are some other two-part sentences:

Although Julie loves chocolate, she rarely eats it.
Julie rarely eats chocolate although she loves it.
When I get home, I'll take a nap.
I'll take a nap when I get home.

However and *although* are often used with similar meaning, but they need different punctuation.

She didn't study. However, she passed the course.
She passed the course although she didn't study.

- Certain verb forms can't be the only verb in a sentence.

Verbs ending in *-ing* usually continue sentences. Watch out for fragments like these:

Leaping across the hot sand.
One being my cousin.
The sun setting over the prairie.

One solution is to connect the fragment to the preceding sentence.

They ran towards the ocean, leaping across the hot sand.

The second solution is to change the *-ing* verb to a complete verb.

They leaped across the hot sand.
One is my cousin.
The sun was setting over the prairie.

To verbs (*to be, to feel*) also frequently begin fragments.

I went back home to talk to my father. To tell him how I feel.

Fix this fragment by joining it to the previous sentence or adding a sentence starter:

I went back home to talk to my father, to tell him how I feel.
I went back home to talk to my father. I needed to tell him how I feel.

To verbs and *-ing* verbs *can* begin sentences if a complete verb comes later.

The sun setting over the prairie is my favorite memory.
To talk to my father always calms me down.

- *That* starts a sentence when it points.

  That man is my uncle.
  That is a good machine.

  Otherwise, *that* is a sentence connector.

  I believe that you are a good friend, that I can count on you.

- A repeated word can create a fragment.

  Elizabeth's the ideal cat. A cat who both plays and purrs.

  The best solution here is to replace the period with a comma.

  Elizabeth's the ideal cat, a cat who both plays and purrs.

You will notice that professional writers sometimes use sentence fragments for emphasis or style. Be sure you have control over fragments before you experiment. In the right spot, fragments can be very strong.

COMMAS

You don't need a comma every time you breathe. Here are four places you need them.

- Put a comma before *and, but, so,* and *yet* when they connect two sentences.

  The roads are slick, but you can make it.

  However, don't automatically stick in a comma just because a sentence is long.

  The short man wearing red shoes and pink socks is my uncle Jules.

- Use commas between parts of a series of three or more.

  I bought Perrier, Wheat Thins, and Velveeta for my party.

  In the class sat a bearded man, a police officer, a woman eating a sandwich, and a parakeet. (Without the comma, what happens to the parakeet?)

  Don't use a comma in a pair.

  I bought Perrier and Velveeta.
  The tall man in a suit and the woman in a dress were husband and wife.
  We went swimming in the afternoon and ate out in the evening.

- Use a comma after a lead-in to a sentence.

  However, Kathryn proved him wrong.
  Instead, he went to Philadelphia.
  For example, Larry built his own house.
  If we had left on time, we would be there by now.
  After we got home, she gave me a cup of that terrible herb tea.

- Surround an insertion or interruption with a *pair* of commas.

My cousin, who thinks she is always right, was dead wrong.
Billy, of course, won the election.
I told Susan, the neighbor, all about the baby.
Frank, even though he didn't practice, won first prize.

These are wrong if you use only one comma—double or nothing.

Places and *dates* are treated as insertions.

I was born on August 15, 1954, at seven in the morning.
The hospital was in Oshkosh, Wisconsin, not far from Omro.

SEMICOLONS AND COLONS

Semicolons can be used instead of periods; they also can separate parts of a complicated list. Colons create suspense: they set up a list, a quotation, or an emphatic statement.

SEMICOLONS

- Use a semicolon instead of a period to connect two related sentences; each half must be a complete sentence.

He was fat; she was thin.
Hope for the best; plan for the worst.
I'll never forget the day of the circus; that's when I met the trapeze artist who changed my life.

Semicolons usually come before certain transition words:

however	therefore
nevertheless	in other words
for example	on the other hand

Schubert was a great composer; however, Beethoven was greater.

- Use semicolons instead of commas in a list when some of the parts already have commas.

To make it as an actor or actress, you need, first of all, some natural talent; second, the habits of discipline and concentration; and third, the ability to promote yourself.

COLONS

Use a colon after a complete statement to introduce related details.

Before a colon you must have a *complete statement*. Don't use a colon after *are* or *include* or *such as*.

Colons can introduce

- A list

  I came home loaded with supplies: a tent, a sleeping bag, and a pack.

- A quotation

  The author begins with a shocker: "Mother spent her summer sitting naked on a rock."

- An example

  I love to eat legumes: for example, beans or lentils.

- An emphatic assertion

  This is the bottom line: I refuse to work for only $5.00 an hour.

Use a colon before a subtitle.

  Pablo Picasso: *The Playful Artist*

When you type, leave two spaces after a colon.

DASHES AND PARENTHESES

Dashes and parentheses separate a word or remark from the rest of the sentence.

Dashes highlight the part of the sentence they separate, or show an abrupt change of thought in mid-sentence, or connect a fragment to a sentence.

Alberta Hunter—still singing at the age of eighty—performed nightly at The Cookery in New York City.

At night the forest is magical and fascinating—and yet it terrifies me.

Living the high life—that's what I want.

Dashes are very handy; they can replace a period, comma, colon, or semicolon. However, they are usually informal, so don't use many—or you will seem to have dashed off your paper.

When you type, two hyphens make a dash; do not space before or after the dash.

Parentheses de-emphasize the words they separate. Use them to enclose brief explanations or interruptions. They can contain either part of a sentence or a whole sentence.

We demanded a reasonable sum ($100 an hour) for our work.

Mayme drives slowly (she claims her car won't go over 40 miles per hour), so she gets tickets for causing traffic jams.

Archie marched into the room and (are you ready for this?) began to spray the walls hot pink.

Polly's last movie disappointed both fans and critics. (See the attached reviews.)

If the parentheses contain part of a sentence, put any necessary punctuation after the second parenthesis. If the parentheses contain a sentence all by itself, put the period inside the second parenthesis. (Notice, however, that when parentheses enclose a sentence within a sentence, you don't capitalize or use a period.)

Be sparing with parentheses. Too many can chop up your sentences.

HYPHENS

Hyphens are used to join two words or to divide a word at the end of the line.

- Hyphens join compound words.

  self-employed
  in-laws

- Hyphens make a two-word adjective before a noun, but not after it.

  Maggie has a high-paying job.
  Maggie's job is high paying.

- A hyphen can divide a multisyllable word at the end of a line. Divide only long words and only between syllables. When in doubt, do not divide.

QUOTATION MARKS

Use quotation marks any time you use someone else's exact words. If they are not the exact words, don't surround them with quotation marks.

Punctuation before a Quotation

Here are three ways to lead into a quotation:

- For short quotations (a word or a phrase), don't say *Twain says,* and don't put a comma before the quotation. Simply use the writer's phrase as it fits smoothly into your sentence:

  Huck Finn finds it "lovely" to float down the Mississippi River on a raft.

- Put a comma before the quotation marks if you use *he says.* Put no comma if you use *he says that.*

  Mark Twain says, "It's lovely to live on a raft."
  Mark Twain says that "It's lovely to live on a raft."

- Use a colon (:) before a quotation of a sentence or more. Be sure you have a complete statement before the colon. Don't use *he says.*

  Twain romanticizes Huck's life on the river: "It's lovely to live on a raft."

Punctuation after a Quotation

At the end of a quotation, the period or comma goes *inside* the quotation marks. Do not close the quotation marks until the person's words end.

> Twain says, ". . . you could hear a fiddle or a song coming over from one of them crafts. It's lovely to live on a raft."

Semicolons go outside of closing quotation marks.

> Huck says, "It's lovely to live on a raft"; however, this raft eventually drifts him into trouble.

Question marks and exclamation marks go inside if the person is asking or exclaiming. (If *you* are asking or exclaiming, the mark goes outside.)

> "Have you read *Huckleberry Finn*?" she asked.
> Did Twain call Huck's life "lovely"?

When your quotation is more than a few words, let the quotation end your sentence. Otherwise you're liable to get a tangled sentence.

> *Tangled*: Huck says, "It's lovely to live on a raft" illustrates his love for freedom.

> *Correct*: Huck says, "It's lovely to live on a raft." This quotation illustrates his love for freedom.

Indenting Long Quotations

Long quotations (three or more lines) do not get quotation marks. Instead, start on a new line and indent the whole quotation ten spaces from the left margin. After the quotation, return to the original margin and continue your paragraph.

Huck and Jim lead a life of ease:

> Sometimes we'd have that whole river all to ourselves for the longest time. Yonder was the banks and the islands, across the water; and maybe a spark—which was a candle in a cabin window—and sometimes on the water you could see a spark or two—on a raft or a scow, you know; and maybe you could hear a fiddle or a song coming over from one of them crafts. It's lovely to live on a raft.

Ellipsis (. . .) means words are left out. Brackets ([ ]) mean you've added or changed a word to make the quotation clear.

> Sometimes we'd have that whole river [the Mississippi] all to ourselves for the longest time. . . . It's lovely to live on a raft.

Note that the fourth dot with ellipsis is a period.

Dialogue

In dialogue, start a new paragraph every time you switch from one speaker to the other.

> "Did you enjoy reading *Huckleberry Finn*?" asked Professor Migliaccio.
> "Well, yes," Joylene said, "but the grammar in it is awful."

Writing about a Word or Phrase

When you discuss a word or phrase, surround it with quotation marks.

> Advertisers use "America," while news reporters refer to "the United States."
> The name "Mark Twain" means "two fathoms deep."

Do not use quotation marks around slang; either use the word without quotation marks, or find a better word.

Quotation within a Quotation

For quotations within a quotation, use single quotation marks:

> According to radio announcer Rhingo Lake, "The jockey clearly screamed 'I've been foiled!' as the horse fell to the ground right before the finish line."

Quoting Poetry

For poetry, when quoting two or more lines, indent ten spaces from the left margin and copy the lines of poetry exactly as the poet arranged them.

> . . . We are such stuff
> As dreams are made on; and our little life
> Is rounded with a sleep.

When quoting a *few* words of poetry that include a line break, use a slash mark to show where the poet's line ends.

> Shakespeare calls us "such stuff / As dreams are made on. . . ."

UNDERLINING OR QUOTING TITLES

Underline titles of longer works and use quotation marks for titles of shorter works.

- <u>Underline</u> titles of longer works, such as books, magazines, plays, newspapers, movies, and television shows.

  <u>Newsweek</u>
  <u>The New York Times</u>
  <u>War and Peace</u>
  <u>E.T.</u>

  Underlining indicates italics to the printer. Some word processors allow you to use italics instead of underlining.

- Put within "quotation marks" titles of shorter works, such as short stories, articles, poems, songs, and chapter titles.

  "Little Boy Blue"
  "The Star-Spangled Banner"
  "The Pit and the Pendulum"

  Note: Capitalize only the first word and all major words in a title.

- Do not underline or place quotation marks around your title on a cover sheet—unless your title contains someone else's title:

  An Analysis of Frost's "Fire and Ice"
  The Vision of War in <u>The Red Badge of Courage</u>

VERB AGREEMENT

The word before the verb is not always its subject. Look for *who* or *what* is doing the action.

- Remember that two singular subjects joined by *and* (the bird and the bee) make a plural and need a plural verb.

  The bird and the bee make music together.

- Sometimes an insertion separates the subject and verb.

  The drummer, not the other musicians, sets the rhythm.
  The lady who sells flowers has a mysterious voice.

- Sometimes an *of* phrase separates the subject and verb; read the sentence without the *of* phrase.

  One of the guests is a sleepwalker.
  Each of us owns a boat.
  The use of cigarettes is dangerous.

- See what follows *there was, there were, there is, there are.*

  There was one cow.
  There were two cows.

- Words with *one* and *body* are singular.

  Everyone was laughing.
  Somebody always wins.

- Sometimes a group can be singular.

  My family eats crowder peas.
  The team argues after every game.
  A thousand dollars is a lot of money.

- *-ing* phrases are usually singular.

  Dating two people is tricky.

SHIFTING VERB TENSES

Often you find yourself slipping back and forth between present and past verb tenses. Be consistent, especially within each paragraph.

Use the present tense for writing about the story from a book, play, or movie.

Scarlett comes into the room and pulls down the draperies.
Hamlet feels sorry for himself.

Use the simple past tense to tell your own stories.

I lied to the Assistant Principal.
She waved after she boarded the train.

had

Watch out for *had*: You often don't need it. Use *had* to refer to events that were already finished when your story or example took place—the past before the past that you're describing. To check, try adding *previously* or *already*. They can go with *had*.

In 1986, we moved to New York. We had lived in Florida for three years.

(Try adding *previously* or *already* next to *had*.)

would

Most of the time, you can leave out *would*. Use it for something that happened regularly during a period of the past.

The teacher would always make us stand up when she entered the room.

Use *would* for hypothetical situations.

If I were you, I would apologize right now.

could
can

Use *could* to refer to the past and *can* to refer to the present.

Past: Frank couldn't go in the ocean because it was too rough.

Present: Frank can't swim in the ocean because it's too rough.

Use *could* to show what might happen and doesn't; use *can* to show ability.

My parents make good money. They *could* buy us anything, but they don't.

My parents make good money. They *can* buy us anything we want.

gone
eaten
done
seen

Avoid expressions such as *I seen* and *He has went*. Use *gone, eaten, done, seen* after a helping verb.

We went.
I ate.
He did it.
He saw the light.

We have gone.
I have eaten.
He has done it.
She has seen the light.

WORD ENDINGS: S AND *ED*

If word endings give you problems, train yourself to check every noun to see if it needs *s*, and every verb to see if it needs *s* or *ed*.

When to Add ed

- To form most simple past tenses

  She walked.   He tripped.   Mae asked a question.

- After *has, have, had*

  He has walked.   We have talked.   She had already arrived.

- After the *be* verbs (*are, were, is, was, am, be, been, being*)

  They are prejudiced.   She was depressed.   He will be prepared.

Do not add *ed*:

- After *to*   He loved to walk.
- After *would*   Every day he would walk three miles.
- After *did, didn't*   He didn't walk very often.
- After an irregular past tense   I bought bread.
  He found his keys.
  The cup fell.

When to Add s

- To form a plural (more than one)

  many scientists   two potatoes

- To the present tense of a verb that follows *he, she, it,* or a singular noun

  He walks.   It talks.
  She says.   The dog sees the fire hydrant.
  Bill asks.   Polly insists.

  Note: Usually when there is an *s* on the noun, there is no *s* on the verb.

  Pots rattle.

- To form a possessive (with an apostrophe):

  John's mother   today's society
  Sally's house   women's clothing

TANGLED SENTENCES

Look at your sentences to make sure the parts go with each other. Here are the three most common problems.

Parallel Structure

The parts of a list (or pair) must be in the same format.

Not Parallel: I love swimming, to play tennis, and baseball.

Parallel: I love swimming, tennis, and baseball.

   I love to swim, to play tennis, and to play baseball.

Not Parallel: Marty agreed with Fred, with Arnie, and me.

Parallel: Marty agreed with Fred, with Arnie, and with me.

Danglers

There are two problems. In one, a word (often a pronoun) has been left out, so that the introductory phrase doesn't fit with what follows.

Dangler: Dashing wildly across the platform, the subway pulled out of the station.
(This sounds as if the subway dashed across the platform. To correct it, add the missing word—in this case, *we*.)

Correct: As we dashed wildly across the platform, the subway pulled out of the station.

45

The second problem occurs when a phrase or word in a sentence is too far from the part it goes with.

Dangler: A former athlete, the reporters interviewed Terrence Harley about the use of steroids.
(This sounds as if the reporters are a former athlete.)

Correct: The reporters interviewed Terrence Harley, a former athlete, about the use of steroids.

Mixed Sentence Patterns

Sometimes you start with one way of getting to a point, but one of the words slides you into a different way of saying it. The two patterns get mixed up. Correct a mixed sentence pattern by using one pattern or the other.

Mixed (Incorrect):   By opening the window lets in fresh air.
(Here the writer started to say "By opening the window, I let in fresh air," but the word *window* took over.)

Correct: By opening the window, I let in fresh air.

Correct: Opening the window lets in fresh air.

Re-read your sentence as a whole to make sure that the end goes with the beginning.

MEETING SPECIFIC ASSIGNMENTS

P·A·R·T II

FORMAT OF COLLEGE PAPERS

Paper

- Use 8 1/2" × 11" paper—not that sticky, erasable paper.
- Use one side of the paper only.
- Staple once or clip in the upper left-hand corner.
- If you type on a computer, remove perforated edges.

Spacing

- Double space between lines.
- Use an inch to an inch-and-a-half margin on all four sides.
- Indent each paragraph five spaces.
- At the bottom of the page, use a full last line, unless you're ending a paragraph. It's all right to end a page in mid-sentence.

Spacing after Punctuation

- Leave two spaces after
    Periods
    Question marks
    Exclamation marks
    Colons

- Leave one space after
    Commas
    Semicolons
- Make a dash by using two hyphens—with no space before or after.
- Make ellipsis (. . .) by using three periods with a space between each.
- Never begin a line with a period or a comma.

Page Numbers

Number each page after the first.

Cover Sheet

- The title, without quotation marks or underlining
- Your name
- The date
- The course title and number
- The teacher's name

Center the title in the middle of the page and put the other information in the lower right-hand corner.

DIVIDING WORDS

Avoid, as much as possible, dividing words from one line to the next. If a word has five letters or fewer, fit it on one line or the other.

Divide only between syllables.

- To find the syllables, look up the word in a dictionary. It will be printed with dots between the syllables: *gua·ran·tee.*
- Never divide a one-syllable word, like *brought.*
- Never divide a word after only one letter.

SOME ADVICE ABOUT TYPING

You'll need to hand in many typed papers in college, so it pays to learn to type or use a word processor. If you don't have a computer, most colleges and many public libraries have a computer room where you can take your own disk and type and print out your paper.

If, however, a friend or relative types for you, be sure that the typist doesn't interfere with the content. Don't let someone else tell you how to do your assignment.

A WORD ABOUT PROOFREADING

No matter who has typed your paper, you must read the typed copy several times. A typo counts as an error; it's no excuse to say, "Oh, that's just a typo."

Often teachers don't mind if you correct your typed copy with a pen. If it's okay, you can draw a line through the word you wish to change and write the correction above the line. Small corrections can also be made with correction fluid. If you use a word processor, proofread your paper both on the monitor and on the printout. Don't rely solely on a spelling checker; it will miss errors like *to* for *too.*

TAKING NOTES IN CLASS

Some students take too many notes. They confuse *note-taking* with *writing* and try to get down every word. At the end of class, their wrists are limp and they haven't heard a word.

Some students don't take enough notes. When the time comes to study for a test, they have only a few odd notes copied from the blackboard—not enough to make sense.

Here are a few pointers:

Listen Far More than You Write

Listen for lead-in phrases, like, "The most important . . ."; listen for ideas the teacher repeats. After you are certain you've heard a whole unit of thought, then jot down some notes.

Write Short Notes in Outline Form

Don't write down complete sentences; use one or two words or significant phrases, enough to remind you of what was covered. If page numbers from the text are referred to, jot the numbers down to check later.

Use Plenty of Paper

Leave plenty of white space between major headings. Most lecturers backtrack as they remember ideas or shoot ahead of themselves and then return to the current topic. They are talking, creating the ideas as they go.

Go Over Your Notes As Soon As Possible After Class

While your memory is fresh, re-read and fill in your notes.

Before the Test, Make a Condensed Version of Your Notes

Mark all the important points in your notes with an asterisk or with highlighting pens. Make a brief outline. If you can, type it up—again leaving plenty of white space so you can go back and add details.

ESSAY TESTS: HOW TO OVERCOME PANIC AND PRESSURE

A wave of panic—that's what most people feel when they are handed an essay test. Some students, feeling the pressure, plunge in and write the first thoughts that come to mind. But your first thoughts aren't necessarily your best thoughts. There's a smarter way to write an essay exam.

Take Your Time at the Beginning

- Sit and jot down brief notes for a few minutes. Don't write whole sentences yet—just a word or phrase for each idea, example, or fact.
- Re-read the question and instructions carefully. Be sure you're writing what you've been asked for.
- Take a few more minutes to expand your notes. Stay calm. Don't start writing too soon.
- Subdivide your answer into two or three parts and stick to them.

Write a First Sentence Which Uses Words from the Question and Tells the Parts of Your Answer

There were three causes of the sudden population increase in eighteenth-century Europe: first, the new wealth gathered from colonies; second, a decrease in European wars; and third, the discovery of the potato as a cheap food source.

Plan Your Paragraphs

- For a short essay—one paragraph
  Write your introductory sentence followed by three facts which support it. Explain one part at a time—in order—to make a full paragraph.
- For a long essay
  Write your introductory sentence as a paragraph by itself.
  Then give each point a paragraph. Restate the point, explain what you mean by any general words, and give facts or examples to prove your point.
  Write a brief conclusion, stressing what's most important.

Don't Start Over

- Stick to your plan. If you get a new idea, use an asterisk (*) or an arrow to show where it goes.
- Leave room after each paragraph for ideas you might want to add later. If you are writing in an exam booklet, write on only one side of the page so that you will have room for insertions.
- If you add or cut a main point, go back and revise your introduction to match the change.

Don't Pad Your Answer

- Use a direct, no-nonsense style. Don't try for big words—they just lead to errors when you are under time pressure. Simply state your points and the facts to back them up, one step at a time.

Don't Make a Neat Copy

Copying over wastes precious time, and the copy tends to be full of slips and errors. Instead, put a line through an error and correct it above the line; use a carat (∧) for a short insertion, an asterisk (*) or arrow for a long insertion.

Don't Rush at the End

- Stop writing ten minutes before the end of the test.
- Re-read your essay for content. Don't add to it unless you find a *major* omission. Late additions usually create errors and disorganization.
- Proofread, with special attention to the second half of the essay (where rushing leads to errors) and to the very first sentence. Look for words like *to* and *too, then* and *than*. Check your *periods* to be sure you have no run-on sentences or fragments. Look carefully to make sure that you haven't left out any words or letters.

USING THE COLLEGE LIBRARY

When you are searching for information, there's no better place to begin than the college library. Familiarize yourself with all these resources:

Card Catalogs

Books, media holdings, reference materials are catalogued by

author

title

subject

Whereas most public and high school libraries use the Dewey Decimal System, college and university libraries use the Library of Congress Classification System. This system separates all knowledge into twenty-one classes, each identified by a letter or letters of the alphabet, followed by numbers. These letters and numbers are the *call number* and are located at the top of each card in the catalog. You need the complete call number in order to locate a book. It also helps to copy down the author and title.

Note: Many libraries also have their card catalogs on a computer.

Stacks

These are the rows of books that take up most of the space on every floor. In order to find a book you want, you have to have the exact call number. If the book's not there, you can ask at the circulation desk if it's checked out and, if it is, put your name down to receive it when it's returned. The library will notify you when it comes back in.

The Reserve Room

This is the section in the library where you go to check out, for a few hours or overnight, books and other materials that your teacher has put aside for class.

Reference Section

Materials in this section are usually encyclopedias, dictionaries, and special collections of information. You can use them only in the library.

Periodicals Section (or Index Room)

Here's where you find annual indexes to newspapers, magazines, and journals. *The Reader's Guide* and *The Magazine Index* list all subjects covered in popular magazines. *The New York Times Index* lists subjects covered in *The New York Times* each year. Other indexes are more specialized; ask the librarian for help. List the periodicals and pages you want and check the holdings file, the list of magazines your library carries. Sometimes you can get a copy of the magazine itself from the circulation desk; most of the time, especially for newspaper articles, you will have to read copies on microfilm or microfiche.

Microfilm/Microfiche Room

A separate area houses reading machines and drawers full of microfilm and microfiche. Each slide or roll of film contains hundreds of pages of newspapers or magazines. Someone is usually there to help you use the machine the first time; after that, it's easy. You can make a copy of any page you want, often on the machine itself.

The Pamphlet File

Somewhere in every library is the "pamphlet file" (sometimes called the "vertical file" or "clip file"). In this file are housed years and years of clippings, accumulations of pamphlets—all sorts of information about any subjects the librarians thought important. This is an especially good source of information for material pertaining to local areas such as your state or home town.

Media Section

Here you can see slides, filmstrips, videotapes; listen to records or compact disks; look at slides under microscopes; and listen to foreign language tapes.

Typewriters and Computers

More and more libraries are providing typing rooms, complete with electric typewriters and, even more recently, computers on which you can type your paper. As more computers enter the scene, centers are being set up within the library itself where instruction in using the machines is provided.

Two Other Important Services

Interlibrary Loan: At your request, the library can obtain copies of books and photocopies of articles from other libraries.

Computer Searches: For a small fee, you can request a computer search in order to identify most sources about a subject field.

WRITING ABOUT READING

HOW TO THINK THROUGH YOUR ESSAY

You will need to be certain of your teacher's expectations. Some teachers want a *summary* of your reading, in which you tell the main points of what you've read, followed by your evaluation. However, most literature teachers want you to stress an important idea about the reading and to demonstrate the details that gave you your idea.

Omit Plot Summary and the Author's Life

Unless you've been asked to, do not include a detailed plot summary which repeats all the points of the reading, or the author's life story. Remember, the teacher already knows what the book says but does not know your ideas about the assignment.

Gather Your First Impressions of the Topic

Begin by freewriting about the question you have been asked or the topic you are considering: Write your first impressions quickly, without pausing, to get your ideas on paper. Do not worry about organization yet; don't even stop to re-read. After ten minutes, read your ideas, underline the most important, and write a sentence to sum up your main idea.

Re-read the Text

Search for evidence to support your main idea, and also
for evidence that might lead you to modify it. The
evidence could include incidents in a story or subtleties of
style. Make notes as you re-read, and mark passages you
may wish to quote.

Organize Your Essay

Do not merely follow the order of what you read. Look at
your original freewriting, and revise your main idea if
necessary. Decide on the parts of your idea and the order
that will make them clear.

Use Evidence to Back Up Your Points

For each main point you make, explain which details from
the reading support the point. In some cases, *briefly* quote
the author. After referring to a detail or quoting a
statement, always explain why that detail or statement
supports your point.

Write a Title for Your Paper

The title should express the main idea of your paper, not
just give the title of the text.

TECHNICALITIES

Titles

<u>Underline</u> titles of books, plays, television shows,
magazines, and newspapers. Put "quotation marks"
around titles of stories, articles, and poems.

Authors

Use the author's full name the first time you mention it. Thereafter, use the full name or last name—not the first name by itself.

Emily Dickinson wrote 1,775 poems.

or

Dickinson wrote 1,775 poems.

Sentence of Identification

Be sure to identify the title and author early in your essay, even if you've already done so in your title.

In "Because I Could Not Stop for Death," Dickinson . . . .
"A Rose for Emily," by William Faulkner, is . . . .
Freud's <u>The Interpretation of Dreams</u> . . . .

Crediting Your Source

If you are quoting from only one source, give information at the end of the paper on the edition you used. List the author, the title, the city of publication, the publisher, and the copyright date. If you want to provide the original date of publication, put it immediately after the title.

Fitzgerald, Zelda. <u>Save Me the Waltz</u>. 1932. New York: Signet-New American Library, 1960.

Directly after each quotation, give the page number in parentheses. For a poem, give the line number.

The novel ends with a couple "watching the twilight" (203).

For more than one source, see "Documentation."

Verb Tense

Use present tense to refer to the story:

Hamlet feels torn by indecision.

HOW TO QUOTE FROM YOUR SOURCES

A good quotation demonstrates the point you are making.

Keep the Quotations Secondary to Your Own Ideas and Words

Each quotation should illustrate a definite point you want to make. Before and after the quotation, stress your point. Maintain your own writing style throughout the paper.

Don't Use Many Quotations

Too many quotations chop up your paper and lead the reader away from your points. Most of the time, tell what you found out in your own style. Instead of quoting, you can *summarize* (give the main points of what you read) or *paraphrase* (explain a single point in detail in your own words).

Keep Your Quotations Brief

Short quotations are the easiest and most graceful to use. Avoid using many quotations of over three or four lines. If you want to use a long quotation, omit sections that do not apply and use ellipsis (. . .) to indicate the part you've left out. A long quotation should be followed by a discussion, in the same paragraph, of the points you are making about the quotation.

Introduce Your Quotations

Direct quotations should usually be preceded by identifying tags. Always make clear who is speaking and the source of the information.

Professor Bigelow says, "Our history is also our destiny."

Incorporating the author's name and any other pertinent information into your text will vary your quotations:

Dr. Trey Porter, an authority in adolescent psychology, maintains that teenagers share a major fantasy: "They all dream of the day they will be free from parental control."

In any case, don't begin a sentence or a paragraph with a direct quotation without an introduction.

Incorporate Each Quotation Into a Clear Sentence

Be certain that your quotations make sense, both in sentence structure and in content. If you use fragments of quotations, be certain that they are woven into complete sentences.

Photographer Michael George states that "wasting film" ultimately saves a photographer time and effort.

WRITING RESEARCH PAPERS

Here it is again, that terrifying request from a teacher for a "research" or "term" paper. Don't be scared by the names of these papers. A research or term paper is simply a fairly long paper in which you set forth a point of view and support it with outside authorities—sources.

Here are some methods for keeping control of your paper:

Before Beginning Research, Freewrite about the Topic

To discover your preliminary main point, write what you already know quickly. Write nonstop for about fifteen minutes without thinking about organization. You can include the reasons you're interested in this subject and questions you'd like to answer.

Write a Controlling Sentence

Before searching for reading materials, spend some concentrated time and energy on writing *one* major sentence that will explain and limit your paper. (Teachers sometimes call this sentence a thesis statement or a topic sentence.) The whole point is to *limit* what you'll attempt to cover; otherwise, you will read yourself into a hole and never get your paper written. You may sometimes have to use two sentences, but try for one.

Pizza is the most wholesome fast food on the American market today.

Search for Supporting Information

The first step is to choose your reading. Go to the library and comb all the resources there. If your subject isn't listed, look under other related subjects. You can also ask someone who knows the field for suggestions about what's best to read. Look for recent articles. Check bibliographies in the backs of books. It can be exciting to follow the leads that you discover as you search for information. Also, don't overlook other sources such as

- Local organizations
- Interviews with experts in the field
- A visit to an institution

- Your family
- Your classmates
- Local libraries
- Businesses

Read and Take Notes

After you've written down a few key questions, focus your reading on answering those questions. Remember that you want to gather supporting information, not copy other people's words. Be aware that you cannot write your paper while taking notes. These must be two separate steps.

- First, write down the details about your source that you will need for your paper.

  For a book: author, title, place of publication, publisher, and date of publication

  For an article: author, title of article, title of publication, date, and pages

  Keeping an index card for each source with all this information is a good idea; then when you type your *Works Cited* you can simply shuffle the cards into alphabetical order.

- Next, take notes *sparingly* as you read. Take notes in phrases, not whole sentences. You will run yourself crazy if you try to take down every word. It's best to

read a number of paragraphs, then summarize them in
your own words. Immediately write the source (author's
last name and page number will do it). If a quotation
strikes you as well said or interesting, copy it word for
word and put quotation marks around it in your notes.
Be accurate in noting the page number, since you'll
need to tell the page where you found your information.

A word about photocopying material: If you find
something very valuable, photocopy it to save time. But
immediately write on the photocopy the publication
information so that you don't forget where it came from.

- As you read, if you get an insight of your own, stop
  and write about it. Remember, this paper should be told
  by a human being—you—and you need to develop your
  own opinions and thoughts about your subject.

Organize Your Material

- Make a short, informal outline—all the major points you
  plan to make, put into a logical arrangement.

- Set aside all books, magazines, and notes. Try, just from
  memory, to write something about each important topic.
  Or simply freewrite again, and see how the key points
  you've freewritten match up with your informal outline.

- Now you can consult your notes. Read them and see
  which notes relate to the main points on your list. You
  may remember a main point you can add to your list.
  See if particular quotations and facts fit any of your
  main points, but don't feel you have to fit in everything
  you've found.

- Avoid merely giving a part of your paper to each source
  you read; instead, give a part to each of the points you
  want to stress.

- After you've put most of your material together in some
  loose way, go back to the sentence you wrote before
  you began your research—the controlling idea. Is this

still your main point? If not, write a new one. Then look over your outline and notes, and cross off those which don't relate to your main idea.

Now Write Your Essay

- Don't try for fancy words and big sentences. Tell what you know, stressing what is most important.

- Anticipate your reader's questions or doubts. Convince the reader of your views—partly with your confident tone, but mostly with facts and references to authorities.

- Do not jam your essay with long quotations. Use brief ones and not many. Your paper should not be more than one-seventh quotation.

- Lead into your quotations or facts; mention the author from whom you got your information. Weave in such expressions as "According to Professor Joseph Campbell, . . ." or "As Freud points out . . . ."

- After each quotation or fact, give its source in parentheses.

- After presenting quotations or facts, make clear how they relate to the point of your paragraph.

Revise Your Essay

Copying over a first draft is not revising. Make sure that each paragraph has one clear point and is logically connected to the paragraphs before and after it. Omit or move information that doesn't fit with a paragraph's main point. This process is simplified if you have access to a word processor.

Edit Your Essay

Use *Rules of Thumb, Part I* to make corrections before you type, and proofread the final copy as well.

PLAGIARISM (Cheating)

Penalties for plagiarism can be severe: failure of the course or expulsion from the college. Unintentional plagiarism is still plagiarism, so be careful and know the rules.

Plagiarism means *writing facts, quotations, or opinions that you got from someone else or from books, articles, movies, television, or tapes without identifying your source.*

To Avoid Plagiarism

- When in doubt, always give credit for a fact, quotation, or opinion taken from a book or other source. This is true even when you use your own wording.

- When you use a writer's wording—even a phrase—always put quotation marks around the writer's exact words.

- Write with your books closed. Do not write with a book or magazine open next to you. Don't go back and forth taking ideas from a source and writing your paper.

- Don't let your sources take over the essay. Tell what you know well in your own style, stressing what you find most important.

DOCUMENTATION

The word *documentation* means that you have added two ingredients to your paper:

Citations of Sources
List of Works Cited

CITATIONS

When you give citations in a paper, you tell specifically where you got a piece of information—in other words, the *source* you used.

When to Give Your Source

You must acknowledge in your paper the source of

- A direct quotation
- A statistic
- An idea
- Someone else's opinion
- Concrete facts
- Information not commonly known

Even if you *paraphrase* (put someone else's words into your own words) or *summarize* (condense someone else's words or ideas), you still must acknowledge your source of the information.

If a fact is common knowledge (George Washington was the first president), you don't have to give your source.

How to Cite Your Source

These days *footnotes* and *endnotes*—with little numbers above the lines—are used less and less. The current trend is to give your source of information in parentheses immediately after you give the information. This system, *parenthetical citation*, is the easiest to use.

Parenthetical Citation

In this system, you put the author's last name and the page number in parentheses immediately after the information:

(Schrambling 125)

Your reader can look at your list of *Works Cited* at the end of your paper to find the complete source.

In the text, it looks like this:

Gourmet cooks specify olive oil with "a greenish cast" (Waters 297).
Some pizza dough is made with eggs and sugar (Daly 377–8).

Notice that there is no p. or comma.

If your citation comes at the end of a sentence, the period goes *outside* the last parenthesis.

When several facts in a row within one paragraph all come from the same page of a source, use one citation to cover them all. Place the citation after the last fact. Do not, however, wait more than a few lines to let the reader know where the fact came from. In any case, the citation must be in the same paragraph as the fact.

Special Cases

- When you have no author, give the first main word of the title.

  ("Frozen" 330)

- If you use the author's name in your text, give only the page number.

  Regina Schrambling's pizza provides an unusual and nutritious alternative (125).

  According to the U.S. Department of Agriculture, one slice has 145 calories (22).

  Note that sometimes the author is an organization.

- When you have two or more books by the same author, use a main word to indicate the title:

  Claiborne chops the mozzarella and adds grated parmesan (<u>International</u> 440).

- When you quote someone who has been quoted in one of your sources, use *qtd. in* (quoted in):

  Julie Wilson, who says her food is "fresh and honest," makes a blue cheese and pear pizza (qtd. in Claiborne and Franey 69).

  In this example Wilson said it, although you found it in Claiborne and Franey.

- If your source is a personal interview, include the person's name in your paragraph and use no parenthetical citation.

WORKS CITED

When you were gathering your material, you may have used a "working *bibliography*," a list of potential sources. However, now that you have written your paper and have seen which sources you actually did use, you must include at the end of the paper a list of *Works Cited*.

There are two major things to remember about a Works Cited page:

- It is an *alphabetized* listing of the sources used—by the authors' last names or (if no author is listed) by the first main word of the title.

- List *only* those sources which you actually cited in parentheses in your paper, and list the whole article or book—not just the pages you used.

Note that the author is listed last name first. Pay special attention to spacing and punctuation: Double space the entire list. Indent the second and third lines five spaces so that the author's name stands out to the left, and end each entry with a period.

- For a book, include
  Author. <u>Title.</u> City: Publisher, date.

  Waters, Alice. <u>Chez Panisse Menu Cookbook</u>. New York: Random, 1982.

- For an article in a magazine, include
  Author. "Title of Article." <u>Title of Periodical</u> Date: Page(s).

  Schrambling, Regina. "Tex-Mex Pizza." <u>Working Woman</u> Feb. 1988: 125.

- For an article in a newspaper, include
  Author (if given). "Title of Article." <u>Title of Newspaper</u> Complete date, section: page(s).

  "Pillsbury's Pizza Unit to Be Sold." <u>New York Times</u> 18 Mar. 1988, Sec. D: 1, 7.

- For an encyclopedia, include
  "Title of Article." <u>Encyclopedia</u>. Year of the edition.

  "Naples." <u>World Book Encyclopedia</u>. 1987 ed.

- For an article or a story in a collection, list the author and article or story first, followed by the title and the editor of the collection.

Daly, Dorothy. "Italian Cooking." <u>Encyclopedia of European Cooking</u>. Ed. Maria Soper. London: Spring, 1962.

(Notice that some books with the title *encyclopedia* are merely large books or collections of articles.)

Special Cases

- For an article or a book with no author listed, use the first main word of the title and alphabetize according to that.

"Frozen Pizza," <u>Consumer Reports</u> May 1986: 327–31.

- For two or more authors, give the last name first for the first author only; use first name first for the other author(s).

Anderson, Jean, and Ruth Buchan. <u>Half a Can of Tomato Paste and Other Culinary Dilemmas</u>. New York: Harper, 1980.

- For additional works by the same author, use three hyphens and a period in place of the author's name and alphabetize the works by title.

Claiborne, Craig. <u>Craig Claiborne's New York Times Video Cookbook</u>. Videocassette. New York Times Productions, 1985. 110 min.

---. <u>New York Times International Cookbook</u>. New York: Harper, 1971.

- For a pamphlet, follow the format for a book. Often an organization is the publisher. Sometimes no author is listed. If the city of publication is not well known, give the abbreviation for the state. Use *n.d.* for *no date*.

<u>Browning Microwave Oven Cooking Guide</u>.   Mahwah, NJ:
　　Sharp Electronics Corporation, n.d.

- For a radio or television program, underline the title of the program. Give the network, if any, then the station call letters and city. Then list the date of the broadcast.

<u>New York and Company</u>.   WNYC, New York City.   20 Apr.
　　1988.

- For a videocassette, list the author or director and the producer, the release date, and the running time.

Claiborne, Craig.   <u>Craig Claiborne's New York Times Video
　　Cookbook</u>.   Videocassette.   New York Times
　　Productions, 1985.   110 min.

- For an interview you conducted, give the person's name and position, the kind of interview (personal or telephone), and the date.

O'Reilly, Kevin.   [Owner, O'Reilly's Pizza Parlor]. Personal
　　Interview.   19 Oct. 1987.

A sample of a Works Cited page follows. It illustrates a variety of sources and therefore is longer than you probably will need.

WORKS CITED

Child, Julia, Louisette Bertholle, and Simone Beck. Mastering the Art of French Cooking. Vol. 1. New York: Knopf, 1966.

Claiborne, Craig. Craig Claiborne's New York Times Video Cookbook. Videocassette. New York Times Productions, 1985. 110 min.

---. New York Times International Cookbook. New York: Harper, 1971.

Claiborne, Craig, and Pierre Franey. "Feasts Against Frost." New York Times 17 Jan. 1988, Sec. 6: 69–70.

Daly, Dorothy. "Italian Cooking." Encyclopedia of European Cooking. Ed. Maria Soper. London: Spring, 1962.

"Frozen Pizza." Consumer Reports May 1986: 327–31.

Gourmet. The Gourmet Cookbook. Rev. ed. 2 vols. New York: Gourmet, 1965.

"Naples." World Book Encyclopedia. 1987 ed.

New York and Company. WNYC, New York City. 20 Apr. 1988.

O'Reilly, Kevin. [Owner, O'Reilly's Pizza Parlor]. Personal Interview. 19 Oct. 1987.

"Pillsbury's Pizza Unit to Be Sold." New York Times 18 Mar. 1988, Sec. D: 1, 7.

Schrambling, Regina. "Tex-Mex Pizza." Working Woman Feb. 1988: 125.

U.S. Dept. of Agriculture. Nutritive Value of Foods. Washington: GPO, 1981.

PUTTING A
PAPER
TOGETHER

P·A·R·T   III

WHAT TO DO WHEN YOU'RE STUCK

Sometimes the ideas don't seem to be there, or you have only two ideas, or your thoughts are disconnected and jumbled. Sometimes it's hard to know where to begin or what shape your writing should take.

Here are some techniques used by professional writers. Try several—some are better for particular writing tasks. For instance, lists and outlines work when you don't have much time (in an essay exam) or when you have many points to include. Freewriting works well when your topic is subtle, when you want to write with depth. You'll find several techniques that work for you.

Freewriting

In this method, you find your ideas by writing with no plan, quickly, without stopping. Don't worry about what to say first. Start somewhere in the middle. Just write nonstop for ten to twenty minutes. Ignore grammar, spelling, organization. Follow your thoughts as they come. Above all, don't stop! If you hit a blank place, write your last word over and over—you'll soon have a new idea. After you freewrite, write one sentence which begins, "The main point I'm making is. . . ." When you've freewritten several times, read your writing and underline the good sentences. These can be the heart of your essay. You can make a list of them and toy with the order of your final essay. Freewriting takes time, but it is the easiest way to begin and leads to surprising and creative results.

Lists and Outlines

Before you write any sentences, make a list of the points you might use in your essay, including any examples and details that come to mind. Jot them down briefly, a word or phrase for each item. Keeping these points brief makes them easier to read and rearrange. Include any ideas you think of in one long list down the page. When you run dry, wait a little—more ideas will come.

Now start grouping the items on the list. Draw lines connecting examples to the points they illustrate. Then make a new list with the related points grouped together. Decide which idea is most important and cross out ideas or details which do not relate to it. Arrange your points so that each will lead up to the next. Be sure each section of your essay has examples or facts to strengthen your ideas.

You're ready to write. You'll see that this system works best when you have a big topic with many details. Although it seems complicated, it actually saves time. Once you have your plan, the writing of the essay will go very fast.

Using a Tape Recorder

If you have trouble writing as fast as you think, talk your ideas into a recorder. Play them back several times, stopping to write down the best sentences. Another method is to write down four or five sentences before you begin, each starting with the main word of your topic, each different from the others. As you talk, use these sentences to get going when you run dry and to make sure you discuss different aspects of your topic.

A Relaxation Technique to Clear Your Mind

Sit up straight in a chair, put your feet flat on the floor, and place your palms on your thighs. Breathe very slowly, feeling the air spiral through your body. Focus on a spot on the floor. Feel each part of your body relax, starting with your feet. Take your time. Listen to the most distant sounds you can hear, the faintest sounds. Take several minutes or more being still, ears open, muscles relaxing, concentrating on your slow breathing. Then take a deep breath and begin to freewrite.

Talking to a Friend

The idea here is for your friend to help you discover and organize *your* ideas—not to tell you his or her ideas. The best person for this technique is not necessarily a good writer, but he or she must be a good listener. Ask your friend just to listen and not say anything for a few minutes. As you talk, you might jot down points you make. Then ask what came across most vividly. As your friend responds, you may find yourself saying more, trying to make a point clearer. Make notes of the new points, but don't let your friend write or dictate words for you. Once you have plenty of notes, you're ready to be alone and to freewrite or outline. If no friend is available, imagine that a friend is there and talk through your ideas.

TIME WASTERS: WHAT *NOT* TO DO

Don't Recopy Repeatedly

Get down a complete first draft before you try to revise any of it. Write on every second or third line so that you can revise easily. Keep a sheet of note paper handy to jot down new thoughts when they occur, and place a number or star to mark the places where you plan to insert new thoughts.

Don't Use a Dictionary or Thesaurus before the Second Draft

Delay your concern for precise word usage and spelling until you have the whole paper written. Then go back and make improvements.

Don't Spend Hours on an Outline

You will probably revise your outline after the first draft, so don't get bogged down at the beginning. Even with long papers, a topic outline (naming the idea for each paragraph without supporting details) is often a more efficient way to organize.

If you use notecards, arrange them according to the paragraph topics they support, rather than copying them onto an outline.

Don't Try to Make Only One Draft

You may think you can save time by writing only one draft, but you can't get everything perfect the first time. Actually, it's faster to write something *approximately* close to the points you want to make, then go back and revise.

Don't Write with Distractions

When you write, you need to focus your brainpower and physical energy. You can be distracted by music, television, or conversation in the background or by being too uncomfortable or too comfortable. Such distractions waste time by diffusing your energy and concentration.

FINDING AN ORGANIZATION FOR YOUR ESSAY

The purpose of your paper is to convince the reader of your point. Your goal in organizing is to produce a sequence of paragraphs presenting your point one step at a time. But there are many ways to reach this goal.

Some people need a long time to think before they begin writing; others can start right away but then must cut some of what they have written. Some people need an outline; others write first and then reorganize when they see a pattern in their writing. Still others begin in the middle or write the parts of their papers out of order.

No method is the "right" one. Do not feel that you have to fit into a set way of working. Some approaches are better for certain topics; some are better for certain people. You should experiment with several methods to discover how you work best. You might remember when you have been pleased with your writing and what approach you used at that time.

When to Use a Formula and When to Make Up Your Own Plan

Sometimes you are given a set format to follow. Sometimes you can discover a pattern that you can repeat for similar assignments. For instance, lab reports often start with the question to be investigated, then describe the experiment to be tried, follow with your observations, and end with your conclusions. After doing one or two, you may be able to stick with a set pattern. This is especially useful for assignments you must do quickly. But **85** for many topics you will need to discover the best plan by making lists of idea and reordering them, or by writing for a while and then reworking what you've written.

When to Adjust Your Plan

The trick to good organization is *reorganization*. No matter whether you start with an outline, no matter what you think when you begin, your topic may well shift and change as you write. You will find that you come up with better ideas, and your emphasis will become clearer. Therefore, you must be ready to abandon parts or all of your original plan. Some minor points may now become major points. Most writers need to make a new plan *after* they finish a first draft.

If, on the other hand, your problem is starting over too often—making too many plans—then you should write a complete first draft before you make basic changes. Don't worry about having the perfect first sentence or paragraph; get down your ideas and only then reexamine them.

In short, work out the best method of organization for you, varying it according to the assignment. In the end, make sure that you know the main point you want the reader to get and that every sentence contributes to making that point clear.

HOW TO WORK ON A SECOND DRAFT

Revision is not just fixing errors. It means taking a fresh look at all aspects of your paper, moving some parts of it, and completely rewriting others. Look at your first draft from the following angles.

The Real Goal of Your Paper

- A big danger is straying from your subject. It's tempting to include good ideas or long examples that are related to your subject but do not support your main point.

- You might find it helpful to write a sentence that begins, "The main point of my paper is. . . ." This sentence does not necessarily go into your paper, but keep it in front of you as you revise to make sure that every detail supports your main point. Notice that your *real* point may not be the point with which you started. As you look over your work, decide what you are really saying. You may need to write a new introduction that stresses your real goal.

The Order of Your Points

If you have trouble getting from one point to the next, you may need to omit one point or to move your points around.

- Make a list of your points in the order you wrote them.

- Now play with the order so that each one logically leads to the next.

- Get rid of points that aren't related.

- Cover some points briefly as parts of other points.

Make sure that the steps of your thinking are clear, complete, and logical.

Strong Parts and Weak Parts

- Build up what's good. When we revise, we tend to focus on the weak spots. Instead, start by looking for the good parts in your paper. Underline or highlight them, and write more about them. Add examples. Explain more fully. You may find that you have written a new, much better paper.

- Fix up what's bad. Now look at the parts that are giving you trouble. Do you really need them? Are they in the right place? If you got tangled up trying to say something that you consider important, stop and ask yourself, "What is it I'm trying to say, after all?" Then say it to yourself in plain English and write it down that way.

Reading Aloud to a Friend

- When you read your paper to a friend, notice what you *add* as you read—what information or explanations you feel compelled to put in. Jot down these additions and put them into the paper.

- Ask your friend to tell you what came through. All you want is what he or she heard—not whether it's good, not how to change it. Then let your friend ask you questions. However, don't let your friend take over and tell you what to write.

Final Touches

- Look again at the proportions of your paper. Are some of the paragraphs too short and choppy? Is there one that is overly long?

- Look at your first and last paragraphs. You may find that your old first paragraph is no longer your real point. If so, write a new one. Play with the first and last sentences of your paper in order to begin and end with the strongest statements that you can. For an important sentence, write the idea three or four different ways— with very different wording—then choose the best.

- Write a title that catches the reader's attention and that announces your subject.

- Proofread your paper closely several times and make corrections. Watch especially for errors in any of the new material you've written.

HOW TO MAKE A PAPER LONGER (AND WHEN TO MAKE IT SHORTER)

Adding words and phrases to your paper makes it at most an inch longer. Adding new points or new examples will make it grow half a page at a time. There are times, however, when cutting a little bit will make your whole paper stronger.

How to Make a Paper Longer

- Add an example or explain your reasons to demonstrate your point—or even add a new point.

- Mention other views of the subject that differ from yours: either incorporate them (showing the evidence for them) or disprove them (telling why others might accept them and why you reject them).

- Add details (facts, events that happened, things you can see or hear). Details are the life of a paper. Instead of saying, "We got something to drink," say "We swiped a Dr. Pepper from Tom's cooler."

- Expand your conclusion: Discuss implications and questions which your paper brings to mind.

  BUT

- Don't add empty phrases, because they make your writing boring. Don't fake length by using fat margins or big handwriting.

When to Make a Paper Shorter

- Sometimes you think a point is necessary, but when you read your paper to a friend, you notice that you both get bored in that section. Or sometimes you get tangled up trying to make a point clear when you can cover it briefly or cut it entirely. Condense minor points.

- Watch your *pace* when you tell a series of events. Head toward the main point or event directly. Don't get lost in boring preliminary details.

- Avoid getting sidetracked. The digression may interest you, but it may not add to the real point of the essay.

INTRODUCTIONS AND CONCLUSIONS

Beginnings and endings of everything, including written essays, demand special attention. After you've written your paper, pretend that you are a reader leafing through a magazine. Would you stop to read your paper? Would you lose interest at the end? Go back and add an introduction that snags a reader's interest and a conclusion that puts what you've written into perspective. To get a memorable first or last sentence, try writing *five* sentences. They can say the same thing, but they should be worded as differently as possible—one long, one short, one plain, one elegant. If you write five, you'll find the one you want.

INTRODUCTIONS

In an essay exam or under time pressure, write the introduction first to indicate the map of the paper. In a longer essay, when you have more time, try writing your introduction *after* you write the rest of the first draft. Often you don't find your real main point until you've written several pages.

Try some of these ideas if you're stuck for an introduction:

Indicate the Parts of Your Essay

This can be done directly or subtly:

> The Civil War had three main causes: slavery, political imbalance, and economics.

> Although Soviet communism and Chinese communism have similarities, the differences are more important.

State Your Position

Start out with a strong statement about where you stand on the subject.

Define a Key Word or Phrase

Introduce a word or idea that is central to your subject and explain or define it.

Start with the Other Side

Tell what you disagree with and who said it. Give their reasons so that you can later prove them wrong.

Tell a Brief Story

You can use a real event or an imagined one, but keep it short.

Raise Questions

Don't string together a lot of questions you don't really expect the reader to answer. Raise one or two significant questions which you then answer in your essay.

Quote an Authority (but not the dictionary)

First write a statement leading up to the quotation. After the quotation, make your point. Steer clear of "Webster says," which is worn out.

Use the News Lead

Journalists are taught to begin with a sentence incorporating *Who, What, When, Where, How,* and sometimes *Why.*

> During the fourteenth century, one-third of Europe's population died of the bubonic plague—in less than three years.

CONCLUSIONS

Don't end your paper with preaching or clichés.

Summarize

Stress your most important points.

Discuss the Future

Speculate on what the future outcome might be—how the information you've presented might affect the future.

Suggest a Solution

Use your own ideas. Present the findings, then come up with a solution *you* think might make a difference.

Quote an Authority

Use a quotation from some well-known person. Show how it applies to your subject, then add your own comment to it as an ending.

Put Your Idea in a Wider Perspective

What is the importance of what you've said for other people?

Raise Further Questions or Implications

Which issues now remain?

PARAGRAPHS— LONG AND SHORT

The paragraphs of your essay lead the reader step by step through your ideas. Each paragraph should make one point, and every sentence in it should relate to that one point. Usually the paragraph begins by stating the point and then goes on to explain it and make it specific.

Paragraphs should be as long as they need to be to make one point. Sometimes one or two strong sentences can be enough. At other times you need nine or ten sentences to explain your point. However, you want to avoid writing an essay that consists of either one long paragraph or a series of very short ones. Paragraphs give readers a visual landing, a place to pause; so use your eye and vary the lengths of your paragraphs.

Indent the First Word of the Paragraph

In college papers, indent the first word of each paragraph *five* spaces if typing, and approximately that amount of space if you are writing by hand. In business letters or reports, where you single-space between lines, omit the indention and double-space between the paragraphs to divide them.

Break Up Long Paragraphs

A paragraph that is more than ten sentences usually should be divided. Find a natural point for division, such as

- A new subject or idea
- A turning point in a story
- The start of an example
- A change of location or time

Expand Short Paragraphs

Too many short paragraphs can make your thought seem fragmented. If you have a string of paragraphs which consist of one or two sentences, you may need to *combine, develop,* or *omit* some of your paragraphs.

Combine

- Join two paragraphs on the same point
- Include examples in the same paragraph as the point they illustrate
- Regroup your major ideas and make a new paragraph plan

Develop

- Give examples or reasons to support your point
- Cite facts, statistics, or evidence to support your point
- Relate an incident or event that supports your point
- Explain a general term
- Quote authorities to back up what you say

Omit

If you have a short paragraph that cannot be expanded or combined with another, chances are that paragraph should be dropped. Sometimes you have to decide whether you really want to explain a particular point or whether it's not important to your paper.

Check for Continuity

Within a paragraph, make sure that your sentences follow a logical sequence. Each one should build on the previous one and lead to the next.

Link your paragraphs together with transitions—taking words or ideas from one paragraph and using them at the beginning of the next one.

A Tip

If you keep having trouble with your paragraphs, you can rely on this basic paragraph pattern:

- A main point stated in one sentence
- An explanation of any general words in your main point
- Examples or details that support your point
- The reason each example supports your point
- A sentence to sum up

TRANSITIONS

Transitions are *bridges* in your writing which take the reader from one thought to the next. These bridges are always necessary to link paragraphs together within a paper. Usually the transition between paragraphs comes in the first sentence of the new paragraph. Transitions are also sometimes necessary to link together the sentences within a paragraph.

If you are having trouble with transitions, it may be that your points are out of order. Make a list of your main points and juggle your order so that one paragraph leads logically to the next. Then add transitions which underscore the movement from one point to the next.

Keep your transitions brief and inconspicuous. Here are some choices of transition words you can use to illustrate certain points or relationships:

Adding a Point:	furthermore, besides, finally, in addition to
Emphasis:	above all, indeed, in fact, in other words, most important
Time:	then, afterwards, eventually, next, immediately, meanwhile, previously, already, often, since then, now, later, usually
Cause and Effect:	consequently, as a result, therefore, thus
Examples:	for example, for instance
Progression:	first, second, third, furthermore
Contrast:	but, however, in contrast, instead, nevertheless, on the contrary, on the other hand, though, still, unfortunately
Conclusions:	therefore, to sum up, in brief, in general, in short, for these reasons, in retrospect, finally, in conclusion

FIXING CHOPPY SENTENCES

Short sentences have their place. They can be direct and forceful when you want to dramatize a point. If you're getting tangled in too many words, a few short sentences will often get you through. Nevertheless, too many short sentences can sound like a machine gun, so vary the lengths of your sentences, by combining them or adding details to them.

One option is to combine two short sentences *back-to-back*.

- Put a semicolon between them.

  They wanted black; I wanted pink.
  (Be sure each half is a complete sentence.)

- Put a comma followed by one of these connectors:

but	and	for
or	so	yet
nor		

  They wanted black, but I wanted pink.

- Put a semicolon followed by a transition word and a comma. Here are the most common transition words.

however	for example	meanwhile
therefore	furthermore	nevertheless
instead	in other words	on the other
besides		hand

  They wanted black; nevertheless, I wanted pink.
  They wanted black; however, I wanted pink.

A second option is to *insert* the gist of one sentence inside another:

Choppy: Sheila makes a fine living as a model. She is thin. She has high cheekbones.

Combined: Sheila, who is thin and has high cheekbones, makes a fine living as a model.

The problem with most choppy sentences is that one after another starts with the subject of the sentence—in this case, *Sheila* or *she*. Sometimes you can use *who* (for people) or *which* (for things) to start an insertion. Sometimes you can reduce the insertion to a word or two.

I interviewed Nell Partin, who is the mayor.
I interviewed Nell Partin, the mayor.

Third, you can combine sentences by showing a relationship of *time* or *cause and effect*.

Choppy: I got home. I took a nap.

Combined: After I got home, I took a nap.

Choppy: Arthur's check bounced.
               Arthur never balances his checkbook.

Combined: Because he never balances his checkbook, Arthur's check bounced.

               Arthur's check bounced because he never balances his checkbook.

Note that these are two-part sentences. *Because* can start either the first half or the second half of a sentence. Other words that work the same way are *if, although, when, while,* and *whereas*:

Although she didn't study, she aced the exam.
She aced the exam although she didn't study.

If it rains Saturday, we'll have the picnic at home.
We'll have the picnic at home if it rains Saturday.

Sometimes you can lengthen a sentence by adding details.

Short: Billy was popular with the girls.

Longer (and better): Billy, with his slick hair and even slicker talk, was popular with the eighth-grade girls in the back of the school bus.

The best remedy for monotonous sentences is to read your writing out loud and listen for a mix of different lengths. Think of your sentences as music: If you vary them, you can create harmony and rhythm.

PROOFREADING TIPS

Proofreading deserves as much attention as your actual writing. Careless errors undermine what you have said, so make a practice of proofreading several times.

Here are some tips to improve your proofreading:

Make a Break between Writing and Proofreading

Always put a little distance between the writing of a paper and the proofreading of it. That way you'll see it fresh and catch errors you might have otherwise overlooked. Set the paper aside for the night—or even for twenty minutes— while you catch your breath. When you write in class, train yourself *not* to write up until the final moment; give yourself an extra ten minutes before the end of class, take a short break, and then proofread your paper several times before handing it in.

Search for Trouble

Assume that you have made unconscious errors and really look for them. Slow down your reading considerably, and actually look at every word.

Know Your Own Typical Mistakes

Before you proofread, look over any papers you've already gotten back corrected. Recall the errors you need to watch for. As you're writing *this* paper, take ten minutes to learn from the last one.

Proofread for One Type of Error

If periods and commas are your biggest problem, or if you always leave off apostrophes, or if you always write *your* for *you're*, go through the paper checking for just that one problem. Then go back and proofread to check for other mistakes.

Proofread Out of Order

Try starting with the last sentence of the paper and reading backwards to the first sentence; or proofread the second half of the paper first (since that's where most of the errors usually are), take a break, and then proofread the first half.

Proofread Aloud

Try always to read your paper at least once aloud. This will slow you down, and you'll *hear* the difference between what you meant to write and what you actually wrote.

Look Up Anything You're Not Sure Of

Use this book and a dictionary. You'll learn nothing by guessing, but you'll learn something forever if you take the time to look it up.

Proofread Your Final Copy

It does no good to proofread a draft of your paper and then forget to proofread the final paper. This problem crops up often, especially in typewritten papers. Remember: A *typo* is just as much an error as any other error.

With a Word Processor, Proofread on Both Screen and Page

If you are using a word processor, scroll through and make corrections on the screen. Use the spelling checker if there is one, but remember that a spelling checker will not catch commonly confused words like *to* and *too* or *your* and *you're*. You will still need to proofread your printed copy.

WRITING WITH ELEGANCE

P·A·R·T IV

Keeping a Journal
Finding Your Voice
Recognizing Clichés
Trimming Wordiness
Varying Your Sentences
Adding Details
Postscript

KEEPING A JOURNAL

Keeping a journal is one of the best ways to grow as a writer. A journal helps you put your thoughts and feelings into words, helps you overcome writer's block, and helps you develop your own personal style. You will also discover truths you didn't know—about yourself and about many topics. Some of your journal writing can later be developed into complete essays or stories.

Make your journal a record of your inward journey. Don't make it a diary—a day-by-day description of what you do. Instead, set down your memories, your feelings, your observations, your hopes. A journal gives you the opportunity to try your hand at different types of writing, so aim for variety in your entries.

Some Guidelines for Keeping a Journal

- Write nearly every day for at least ten minutes.

- Put each entry on the front of a new page with the day and date of the work at the top. Fill the page and continue on the back if you have more to say.

- Use a notebook you really like. Write in ink.

- Choose one topic each day and stick to it. If you have no topic, write whatever comes into your head or choose one of the suggestions from the list given here.

- While you write, don't worry about correctness. Write as spontaneously and as honestly as you can, and let your thoughts and words flow freely. Remember, this journal is for *you*, and it will be a source of delight to you in years to come.

- After you've written, go back immediately and proofread and make corrections. Be certain you've said what you mean.

Some Suggestions for Journal Entries

Blow off steam.

Describe someone you love.

Tell your favorite story about yourself when you were little.

Reminisce about last year.

Respond to a movie, a TV program, a book, an article, a concert or song.

Write a letter to someone and say what you can't say face to face.

Describe in full detail a place you know and love.

Remember on paper your very first boyfriend or girlfriend.

Make a list of all the things you want to do . . . have already done.

Immortalize one of your enemies in writing.

Relate, using present tense, a memorable dream you've had.

Sit in front of a drawing or painting and write down the feelings and images it evokes in you.

Describe yourself in a crowd.

Analyze your most negative characteristic, then your most positive one.

Relate an incident in which you were proud (or ashamed) of yourself.

Describe your dream house.

Capture on paper some object—such as a toy or piece of clothing—that you loved as a child.

Go all the way back: Try to remember your very first experience in the world and describe how it looked to you then.

Write down a family legend.

Re-create your favorite meal, food, or recipe on paper.

Talk about your favorite pastime.

Set down a "here-and-now" scene: Record sensory details right at the moment you're experiencing them.

Go to a public place and observe people. Write down your observations.

Relate your most pressing problem at present.

Describe your very favorite article of clothing, and tell why it means so much to you.

Speculate about the year that's coming. What do you want to achieve?

Take one item from today's newspaper and give your thoughts about it.

Commit yourself in writing to doing something you've always wanted to do but never have.

Explain how you feel about crying . . . laughing . . . fighting . . . singing.

FINDING YOUR VOICE

Often we write the way we think we're supposed to, with big words and fancy sentences. The writing comes out awkward and impersonal. But good writing has the feel of a real person talking.

To find your own voice as a writer, keep these questions in mind when you write:

Am I saying this in plain English?

Are these words that I normally use?

Am I saying what I know to be true instead of what I think others want to hear?

A great technique for developing your own voice is to read your work aloud. If you do it regularly, you'll begin to notice when other voices are intruding or when you are using round-about phrases. In time, your sentences will gain rhythm and force. Reading aloud helps you to remember that, when you write, you are telling something to somebody. In fact, another good technique is to visualize a particular person and pretend you are writing directly to that person.

Good writing is *honest*. Honest writing requires you to break through your fears of what other people might think of you and to tell what you know to be true. Your readers will appreciate the truth, shared with simplicity by a writer who has given the topic attention and has decided what is important.

RECOGNIZING CLICHÉS

A cliché is a *predictable* word, phrase, or statement. If it sounds very familiar, if it comes very easily, it's probably a cliché. Because clichés are predictable, the reader loses concentration when reading them. Think fresh. Use your own five senses to describe something.

Recognize Clichés

The best way to spot clichés is to make a list of all the ones you hear. Clichés fall into groups:

- Comparisons

  Cold as ice
  Drunk as a skunk
  Hot as . . .

- Pairs

  Hot and heavy
  Apples and oranges

- Images

  Raining cats and dogs
  Your room is a pigsty.

- Sayings

  There are other fish in the sea.
  No use crying over spilt milk.

- Lines

  What's a nice girl like you doing in a place like this?
  Haven't I met you somewhere before?

- Phrases

  Madly in love
  Easier said than done

- "In" words

  fantastic
  awesome
  wonderful

This year's new expression is next year's cliché. (Try saying "groovy" to your friends.)

People use clichés when they have to play it safe—making conversation or writing for an unfamiliar teacher. Uncomfortable situations invite clichés—first dates, beginnings of parties, funerals.

Eliminate Clichés

- Often you can simply omit a cliché—you don't need it. The essay is better without it.

- At other times, replace the cliché by saying what you mean. Give the details.

- Look out for clichés in your conclusion; that's where they love to gather.

- Make up your own comparisons and descriptions. Have fun writing creatively from your own viewpoint and sensations.

TRIMMING WORDINESS

Often we think that people are impressed by a writer who uses big words and long sentences. Actually, people are more impressed by a writer who is *clear*.

- Some words sound good but carry no clear meaning. Omitting them will often make the sentence sharper.

experience	proceeded to
situation	the fact that
is a man who	the reason . . . is because
personality	really
in today's society	thing
	something

Wordy: The fire was a terrifying situation and a depressing experience for all of us.

Trim: The fire terrified and depressed all of us.

Wordy: Carmen is a person who has a tempestuous personality.

Trim: Carmen is tempestuous.

Wordy: The reason she quit was because of the fact that she was sick.

Trim: She quit because of illness.

Wordy: Anger is something we all feel.

Trim: We all feel anger.

- Whenever possible, get rid of

It is	There is
It was	There are
	There were

  Wordy: There are three people who influenced my career

  Trim: Three people influenced my career.

- Avoid redundancy—pointless repetition.

  Wordy: He married his wife twelve years ago.

  Trim: He married twelve years ago.

- Tell what something *is*, rather than what it *isn't*.

  Wordy: Ron's apartment is not very neat.

  Trim: Ron's apartment is a mess.

- Replace fancy or technical words, so long as the meaning is not changed. For example, you can replace *abode* with *house* and *coronary thrombosis* with *heart attack* and bring your paper down to earth.

Don't worry that your papers will be too short: For length, add examples and further thoughts. Look at the topic from a different viewpoint. Add points, not just words.

VARYING YOUR SENTENCES

The same idea can be put in many different ways, and every sentence has movable parts. To get more music or drama into your writing, try playing with your sentences.

Write an Important Sentence Several Ways

You can turn a sentence that troubles you into a sentence that pleases you. Instead of fiddling with a word here and a word there, try writing five completely different sentences—each with the same idea. One could be long, one short, one a generalization, one a picture, and so forth. Often you'll find that your first isn't your best. If you play with several possibilities, you'll come up with the one you want. This technique works well for introductions and conclusions.

Give Your Sentences a Strong Ending

The beginning is worth sixty cents, what's in the middle is worth forty cents, but the end is worth a dollar.

I walked into the room, looked around at all the flowers my friends had sent, took a deep breath, and collapsed into a chair in tears.

When the nights grow cool and foggy and the full moon rises after the day's harvest, Madeline, so the story goes, roams the hills in search of revenge.

What Louie received, after all the plea-bargaining and haggling and postponements and hearings, was a ten-year sentence.

Emphasize the Most Important Part of Your Sentence

Highlight the Major Point

Often sentences contain two or more facts. You can show the relationship between these facts so the most important one stands out.

In these examples, two ideas are given equal weight.

> I docked my sailboat, and the hurricane hit.
> Brad lost a contact lens. He had one blue eye and one brown eye.
> I love Earl. He barks all night long.

Here are the same ideas with one point emphasized.

> Just as I docked my sailboat, the hurricane hit.
> Because Brad lost a contact lens, he had one blue eye and one brown eye.
> I love Earl even though he barks all night long.

Notice that the halves of these sentences can be reversed, but the sentence gains strength when the most interesting point comes last.

Tuck In Interrupters or Insertions

Put transitions or minor information into the middle of your sentence.

> He argues, as you probably know, even with statues.
> From my point of view, however, that's a mistake.
> The interior decoration, designed by his cousin, looked gaudy.

Remember to put commas on both sides of the insertion.

Get Rid of Being Verbs

Being verbs like *is* and *are* sap the energy of your writing. They dilute your sentences. Often you can replace *being* verbs with forceful verbs.

Look out for *am, is, are, was, were, be, being, been.*

Especially watch out for *there is, there are, there were, it is, it was.*

Go through your paper and circle all of these limp verbs. Replace them with dynamic verbs. This exercise produces a dramatic difference in any writing. Don't give up easily. Sometimes you will have to rewrite or combine several sentences.

Michael was living in the past.
Michael lived in the past.

It is sad to see how depressed Mary is.
Mary's depression makes me sad.

His walk was unsteady.
He wobbled when he walked.

The woman is beautiful. Her hair is black and curly. Her eyes are green.
The woman's black, curly hair set off her mysterious green eyes.

Save *being* verbs for times when you actually mean a state of being:

She was born on Bastille Day.
I think; therefore, I am.
I am bushed.

Use Parallel Structure

Parallel structure—repeating certain words for clarity and emphasis—makes elegant sentences.

To be honest is not necessarily to be brutal.

David has a love affair with cars, with football, with scuba diving, and with the math teacher's daughter.

Famous quotations are often based on parallel structure.

I came, I saw, I conquered.

—Julius Caesar

To believe your own thought, to believe that what is true for you in your private heart is true for all men—that is genius.

—Ralph Waldo Emerson

Ask not what your country can do for you; ask what you can do for your country.

—John F. Kennedy

Imitate Good Writers

Take a close look at the writings of some of your favorite authors and pick out a sentence or a paragraph that you particularly like. Read it aloud once or twice, then copy it over several times to get the feel of the language. Now study it closely and try to write an imitation of it. Use the sentence or paragraph as a model, but think up your own ideas and words. This exercise can rapidly expand your power to vary your sentences.

ADDING DETAILS

Details give life to your ideas. As you write, you naturally concentrate on your ideas, but the reader will best remember a strong example or fact.

If a teacher asks for "more details," you probably have a generalization with insufficient support. You need to slow down, take *one* idea at a time and tell what it is based upon. You cannot assume that the reader agrees with you or knows what you're talking about. You have to say where you got your idea. This comes down to adding some of the following details to support your point:

Examples

Facts

Logical reasoning

Explanation of abstract words

Ideas are abstract and hard to picture. To be remembered, they must be embodied in concrete language—in pictures, in facts, in things that happened.

For example, here are three abstract statements:

Gloria means what she says.
The scene in the film was romantic.
The paramecium displayed peculiar behavior.

Now here they are made more concrete.

Gloria means what she says. She says she hates television, and she backs it up by refusing to date any man who watches TV.

The scene was romantic. The soft focus of the camera and the violin music in the background heightened this effect.

The paramecium displayed peculiar behavior. It doubled in size and turned purple.

The best writing appeals to our five senses. Your job as a writer is to put down words that will cause the reader to see, hear, smell, taste, or feel exactly what you experienced.

You can sharpen your senses with "here and now" exercises. Observe and write exactly what you see, feel, smell, taste, and hear moment by moment. Expand your descriptions until they become very specific.

I see a white cloud.
I see a white cloud, in the shape of a whale, against a flat blue sky.

I hear a truck.
I hear truck brakes squealing in the distance.

I smell pizza cooking.
I smell spicy pepperoni pizza baking in my uncle's oven.

I taste a potato chip.
The salty potato chip puckers my tongue.

I feel the sun.
The winter sun warms my face.

POSTSCRIPT

You do your best work when you take pleasure in a job. You write best when you know something about the topic and know what you want to stress. So, when you can, write about a topic you've lived with and have considered over time. When you *have* to write about a topic that seems boring or difficult, get to know it for a while, until it makes sense to you. Start with what is clear to you and you will write well.

Don't quit too soon. Sometimes a few more changes, a little extra attention to fine points, a new paragraph written on a separate piece of paper will transform an acceptable essay into an essay that really pleases you. Through the time you spend writing and rewriting, you will discover what is most important to say.

AN INVITATION

Rules of Thumb was written for you, so we welcome your comments about it. Please send them directly to us:

> Jay Silverman
> Elaine Hughes
> Diana Roberts Wienbroer
>
> Department of English
> Nassau Community College
> Garden City, New York 11530-6793

If you would like to purchase individual copies of *Rules of Thumb* directly from McGraw-Hill, please call this toll-free number:

> 1-800-262-4729

ABOUT THE AUTHORS

A graduate of Amherst College and the University of Virginia, Jay Silverman has received fellowships from the Fulbright-Hayes Foundation, the Andrew Mellon Foundation, and the National Endowment for the Humanities. He has taught at Virginia Highlands Community College and at Nassau Community College where he received the Honors Program award for Excellence in Teaching.

Elaine Farris Hughes came to New York City from Mississippi in 1979 to attend a National Endowment for the Humanities seminar at Columbia University. She has taught writing for seventeen years—at Hinds Community College in Raymond, Mississippi, and at Nassau Community College—and has served as a writing consultant for a number of corporations. She is the author of *Writing from the Source*, to be published in 1991.

As Chair of the English Department of Nassau Community College, Diana Roberts Wienbroer hired both Jay Silverman and Elaine Hughes. For six years, she coordinated a department of 150 faculty members. Besides teaching writing for twenty-five years, both in Texas and New York, she has studied and taught film criticism, and is the co-author of *An Easy Guide to Writing on the Computer*.

INDEX

Boldface numbers indicate the major discussion of a topic in entries with multiple page references.